Christine Hollywood

Fragile Islands

Indigo Dreams Publishing

First Edition: Fragile Islands
First published in Great Britain in 2024 by:
Indigo Dreams Publishing
24, Forest Houses
Cookworthy Moor
Halwill
Beaworthy
Devon
EX21 5UU

www.indigodreamspublishing.com

Christine Hollywood has asserted her right under the Copyright, Designs and Patents Act 1988 to be identified as the author of this work.
© Christine Hollywood 2024

ISBN 978-1-912876-90-7

British Library Cataloguing in Publication Data. A CIP record for this book can be obtained from the British Library.

Designed and typeset in Palatino Linotype by Indigo Dreams.
Cover image created by David Williams, cover design by Ronnie Goodyer.
Printed and bound in Great Britain by 4edge Ltd.

Papers used by Indigo Dreams are recyclable products made from wood grown in sustainable forests following the guidance of the Forest Stewardship Council.

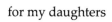

for my daughters

Acknowledgements

I am grateful to the editors of Finished Creatures and Reach Poetry magazines where poems from this collection have been published. Also to the judges of the Indigo Spring Poetry Competition 2023 and Brighton & Hove Poetry Competition 2015 who awarded 2nd place to: Passing Through Richmond Park to Visit My Daughter, and Teatime at The Clarkes respectively.

Thank you to members of Rottingdean Writing Group who looked at early drafts of many of these poems. I am grateful too for feedback and support from Charles Antony, Kate Dyson, John McCullough, Mary Burns and Marion Tracey.

I'd like to thank my friends, and family, who were so very pleased for me and have encouraged and inspired me during the completion of Fragile Islands.

Thank you to Dawn Bauling and Ronnie Goodyer for the opportunity to publish my debut collection with Indigo Dreams.

CONTENTS

Part 1: Judy's Story

Part 2

Fragile Islands

Part 1. Judy's Story

Judy's Story

All through the summer holidays
at 12pm on Weymouth beach,
my husband chucks our baby
in the air and drops it.

The charismatic Mr Punch
in his jester's hat
clouts me
this way
that way round my head
thwacking
with his slapstick
blows to my kidneys,
belly, chest
where it doesn't show
again
and again.

The police turn up,
the doctor
and a crocodile.
He beats them too
and shouts,
That's the way to do it!
in his funny, swazzle voice,
and everybody laughs.

Baby Punch

dear parents
I am primed to love you

cannot tell you
yet

my body
speaks for me

lodged in my skin   my blood   my organs

are the imprints
of the force
you use to throw me

the fact I do not bounce
the way you argue

over me
as your spit
flies
in my face

my hot red yell
unmet   seared
in the beating muscle   of my heart

If You See A Crocodile Don't Forget to Scream!

Some say I represent the devil.
It's true I'm not admired
for my behaviour
or my looks.
If I were less I'd blame my ancestry,
their clumsy clomping,
lack of evolution.
But I know as one of fifty
hatching into life in the soft muddy flatlands
of a hot swampy river
we all have our challenges.
Your mother didn't notice you?
Get over it.

I know I'm lucky.
Take what opportunities I can.
Which leads me onto Punch.
A bit part at first sight –
easy prey
in his stripey onesie –
the man has very little style.
His conduct?
I can't comment

or be called a hypocrite.
You see I am aware of my reputation.
Forget the scaly skin,
small forehead and short limbs,
I am an elite
turbo-charged modern reptile.
My grabber jaws and pincer teeth
do not slide off prey
like some arcade claw machine.

Underwater I'm a beast
and my amber eyes
it has been said
are captivating.
I am a killer
of my own and other species.
No apologies
for using strategies seeded in survival
(and bad mothering)
honed to perfection.

Lurk
Track
Startle
Grab
Tussle Drag
Swirl their limbs off
Drown them
quick.

This doesn't work with Punch.
He mistakes me for a cat –
as if.
Stuffs sausages in my waiting jaws
and beats me with a stick.
The trouble is
we're nowhere near the river.
I'm in his home.
Punch is King.

He triumphs
as I grapple with the sausages.
Not a good look
for a self-respecting crocodile
to be bested by a man
wearing his pyjamas.

Of course they love it.
I am a beast
and that's what I deserve –
there's a clash with my reality.

I hunker down.
Adapt.
Let Punch take centre stage.
Watch
as he takes a long low bow
each time.
And farts loudly at us all.

The Police Inspector and Mr Punch Shake Hands

Evening Mr Punch
        Inspector! Good to see you.
I'm here on business Paul, do you mind if I come in?

        Of course Greg. That was a blinder you played on Saturday.
        Mind the pram and the new baby.
        There's Judy – a little overwrought today, aren't you my love?
        Darling, while I speak to Greg, would you bring us both a tot of
        whisky?
        Judy! Please don't shout!

Judy, is everything alright?
Is the baby not sleeping?
Never mind, you'll soon be back to normal.
I'll only keep him for a minute.
Now Paul, no need for whisky.
Let's hurry through,
then you get back to Judy.

        Follow me, Greg.
        Now what can I help you with?

Paul, please close the door.
First of all, congratulations
on the new addition.
I know what a good man you are,
a valued member of our community,
not to mention a generous supporter
of our own Police Fund.

So I'm here to let you know
there's been a report…of a disturbance.

Your neighbour on the left
has seen the baby being dandled
from a window.
Heard screaming from your wife.
Sounds of beating.
Footsteps running,
followed by a man shouting,
a woman wailing?

All this is off the record Paul,
for your information.
A friendly chat between us,

> *Greg, you've just seen my wife is suffering*
> *with her mental health.*
> *She cries, lashes out, nothing is right*
> *with me or the baby.*
> *I comfort her, and she begins to shout*
> *hurtful, embarrassing stuff about me,*
> *and everyone I know – you included!*
> *Then there's the baby wailing,*
> *because his mother is unwell and cannot feed him properly,*
> *and I'm dashing in between them.*
>
> *This must be what the neighbour heard.*
> *An older lady, lonely, nosey, lives with cats,*
> *you know the sort.*

Paul, I understand.
I'll visit your neighbour on my way back.
Put her in the picture,
tell her about the baby –
you were holding it for her to see!

So Judy's a bit unsettled – it will pass.
Hormones play havoc
with a woman's brain.
I'd call the doctor,
get her on some medication,
you know, improve her mood,
make your life a little easier.

(They laugh together.)

You have it all in hand, I see.
This goes no further, Brother.

The Dr's Notes

Pt's husband requested urgent visit for his wife concerned
about her mental health – says she's listless, prone to outbursts
and attacks him with a stick. On arrival Pt was crumpled in a corner.
Pale with bruising on both arms. When asked about the bruises
Pt said she was so tired she had fallen down the stairs.
B/P & heart rate normal. Baby 6 months. Appears well but crying
through the night. Husband says wife is blaming him for everything,
"causing mayhem" in the home. Discussed hormonal changes/
effect on mental health/need for rest and healthy diet/adjustment
after baby's birth/support. No family nearby. Pt says she's lost
contact with her friends. Encouraged Pt to mix with other mothers,
attend clinics when they run, get out and exercise. Continue
with Kegels to strengthen pelvic floor. If no improvement
in 2 weeks suggest CBT (subject to availability)
or antidepressants (short course). Husband present throughout.

Fragile Islands

Part 2

The Longing of Kangaroos

He wanted to press his face close to the mesh,
peer at their boxy faces, watch them lolloping
on springy back legs.

He hoped he'd see a baby roo
or two, peeking from pouches.
But the day he visited London Zoo
the kangaroo pen was empty.

The door to their hut hung open.
A sign reading, *Red Kangaroos,*
gave no indication of their whereabouts.

He knew they'd left for Australia.
Felt their relief as they leapt
into the wild interior, bounding
mile upon mile of the parched landscape,

kickboxing along the way.
In the day they'd dig deep ditches,
not to get to England but to rest in.

Lying on their sides,
heads on their hands, like we do sometimes,
not thinking of freedom or belonging.

Kids

gallop the yard
on tiny hooves
like pointe shoes

wobbly
they topple
spring up

peer nosily
into buckets
clamber on tree stumps

do you want to hold one
my friend's Dad asks
and plonks a brown baby goat

into my lap
I clasp its barrel chest
silky fur expanding

contracting with its breaths
feel its heart beating
as quickly as my own

Laughing At The Sky

Over the Ashford Road
past the garage and the Yeoman pub,

a tangle of apple trees and brambles.
Our parents told us not to go there

but sometimes
we would dash along the edge,

sometimes in between the trees,
to the pool of slimy green

in a basin of mud, where a boy yelled
he'd seen a man's leg sticking out.

Each time we dared
we'd take turns to peer over the edge,

shout at branches bent like limbs,
point at ripples,

as if the man might suddenly
stagger up and chase us.

Shrieking, our feet tripping
over each other

we'd rush towards the churchyard
and collapse on bumpy grass,

holding our sides in stitches,
laughing at the sky.

Teatime at The Clarkes

When Mr Clarke
calls my aunty fat,

time ticks slowly
on the big clock.

The sun throws shadows
round the sundial.

Red admirals freeze
with their wings shut tight,

flying ants crawl into cracks
and cacti prickle.

Mrs Clarke pours scalding tea
and teacups in their saucers wobble,

and no one
has an appetite for cake.

Creosote

Someone wrote
what was it – piss, bollocks, bum –
in big chalk letters

on the fence
around your school.
Remember the kerfuffle

when the nuns saw?
His Mum is reminiscing
at the family home on Canvey.

He laughs, lets slip
in a jokey kind of way now he's in his thirties,
it was him.

Her forehead cross-hatched,
lips a folded line,
she reaches for her Marlboros.

Blue Light

I think I just forgave Stacy Pummell,
my friend told me.
What that bitch? I replied.

Yeah, last week my counsellor asked me,
Do you think you could forgive her?
And I heard myself say, maybe I can.

<u>Maidstone Technical High School for Girls.</u>
Stacy is looking down her sneering nose, waving it from side to side
as she wanders towards her prey. Her tiny eyes fixed, she flicks
her two foot tongue, slurps up the soundless worms and beetle larvae
she feeds on. The classroom stinks of sweat.

Stacy's an anteater. She's got the biggest claws. The scratchiest fur.
Her legs are so muscly they can fend off lions. Some teachers
like anteaters. Miss Fox our form tutor, gives Stacy and her stoat friend
Gina most of her attention.

There's this treatment for trauma, my friend continues.
A small blue light that moves from side to side
in front of my eyes,

Does it work?
I notice her eyes haven't filled with tears
as usual, when she remembers Stacy.

Well, when I think about her now,
I don't want to find out where she lives,
go round her house, shout in her face,
and punch her.

Tilting

It's 5pm mid-February in the fields
behind the houses.
In the west a terracotta kiln
is sending flares into the sky.

The rest is streaked in pink
and orange pastels.
Photogenic backdrops
turning branches black.

In the fields behind the houses,
new homes are moving nearer.
Paths that led through trees
and marsh and grazing

now have gardens backing on to them.
Windows squint at tracks
sniffed by dogs, ambled by walkers,
home to badgers and wild violets.

In the fields next to the houses,
blackbird, thrush and robin
are singing out their boundaries,
like they know they're on the up.

The moon is glowing like a teenage girl.
At the house the owners are extending,
all the rooms are lit. In the kitchen,
shapes of children dance like fireflies.

Cupcake

Emerging from the corner shop with a four-pack
of cupcakes as I walked past he asked,
Would you like one?

He was the sharpest dressed, best looking boy
amongst the terraces of Clapham South,
the concrete of grey housing blocks.

Undoing the cellophane packaging, placing
the cupcakes on top of the box,
he held them out to me.

Thick orange, lemon, chocolate and strawberry icing
on fluffy vanilla sponge, in soft paper-lined, silver foil cups.
Of course I said *Yes*, extracting the lemon one – my favourite

– and nibbling the icing edge.
He took a bite from the chocolate one then held it out to me,
as he moved round to take a mouthful of mine.

At the top of Dalglish Road, London SW12 in May that year,
we moved closer, glancing at each other's eyes,
the sounds of Saturday around us,

sweetness
           exploding
                        in our mouths.

Falling back against a garden wall we toppled over
onto a patch of grass bordered by alyssum and petunias.
Not that we noticed, consumed

in finding icing in the folds of our clothes,
licking fluffy crumbs from bare arms and shoulders
with the tips of our tongues…   No.

That wasn't what happened.
The only words I found to utter that day –
the day I'd been dreaming about for months – were
No thank you   shyly
                        smiling
of course.

After that we walked along quite awkwardly
while he devoured the chocolate cupcake,
crumbs falling on the unappreciative flatness of the pavement.

As we got to the end of Dalglish Road
he looked sideways at me, scrunched the soft silver paper
into a ball, and as his finger flicked it in the air said,

Bye then.

Everywhere Was Hot That Summer

We're teenagers in London, just left home,
walking dirty pavements oozing heat at 10pm
holding hands, going somewhere.

At the door of The Avalon on Balham High Road
a man in his twenties leans into a pool cue.
Catches eyes with me as we go inside.

I watch as my boy downs his pint in one – it's his trick.
Sip my cider. Look past him, and see the pool-cue man
slowly spreading his upper body

across the green felt of the pool table.
He's rocking the cue between his forefinger and thumb
almost touching its tip to the ball.

Gently he strikes, double kissing it into the pocket.
A fruit machine jangles and reels.
Outside a siren wails.

I Dreamt I Was Paul Simon's Girlfriend

We were getting on okay, early days
it wasn't a relationship – flirtatious though,

I definitely fancied him.
Walking somewhere, following on from something,

I said, *You are rather unusual*
and he said moving closer, our bodies colliding for a second,

You are too.
After that, I was wearing sunglasses and short dresses,

my bare skin glowing in the California heat.
Magazines were full of photos of Paul and me

holding hands and kissing,
announcing our impending wedding.

I was relishing the glamour,
the feeling of melting when I looked into his eyes,

so it didn't seem real
when I woke on the sofa,

the fire blazing,
EastEnders on the TV.

Being Alice

She'd been sunbathing
on the river bank.
Now she was falling down a rabbit hole.
Why had she followed him
with his fast suit and smart chat?

She'd liked his ears,
the humour in his voice,
his flash Rolex.

Tumbling downwards,
too dark to see where she was going,
she glimpsed
a shattered window,
busted door lock,
his curled lip.

She landed.
Her feet scuffing the bottom,
a door half open
in front of her.

It was tiny
and she wasn't going to drink
that potion to shrink
to fit through.
She'd just have to find
another way out.

On Pimlico Road

That day on the number 11,
the side seats by the door,
you were so effusive,
with your green mascaraed eyes,
pink cheeks,

much more familiar
than before
but looking back
I suppose you would be,
you had just
had sex
with my husband.

Breathlessly you chattered
about the weather, school and daughters
and then

the baby said your name,
Jane.

I agreed, *yes Jane.*

The bus stopped
and started
caught in traffic
all the way
to Victoria Station,
where we picked a path
to the school playground,
and waited

for our daughters,
skipping out holding hands.

Tethered

If I made a list of the events that shaped my life
so far, I would write your name in red, highlight in yellow,
underscore.

You were newish to the family,
someone else's partner. We got along ok,
I thought.

When my ex husband called to speak to the children
and said he had spoken to you,
and then began to shout at me,

I asked what you had said to him.
You wouldn't answer, walked away.
I followed – my mistake – asking you to tell me.

You turned, put both your hands
around my throat,
and wrestled me to the floor.

Then you chased us –
me and my two young children –
so we had to bolt the door against you.

The same day or the next
on a bench overlooking the Marina
crouched beneath the undercliff,

the three of us sat stuffing grapes into our mouths,
from a bag we held between us,
watching people park their cars.

I couldn't think what to say to my daughters
about the angry men
I wasn't able to protect them from.

I remember silence starting here,
the loneliness it contained.

You took a place in the family
as though what you'd done
just didn't matter.

Chasms formed.
People and relationships
dropped in.

I tried to find a pattern for the messy shape
that shame began to take in my life.
Visiting my GP I asked,
Could there be something about me
that makes men angry?
He looked at me kindly, and said,
Perhaps.

I folded into myself
a howl,
unheard and tethered
to the undercliff.

Sky

Early summer   on a bench in the garden

chat drifts comfortably between us   I see patches of magenta

someone's left   amber   white

falling remnants of flowers   T-shirts drying in the warm air

magnolia blooms like hankies dangling   I glimpse our long dog

shifting in and out of focus   heat rising from his tongue

things like this keep catching my attention   appearing sideways

                             sometimes full-on

           waving in that space that should be sky

I want to fold them, lay them in a drawer.

Shut.

Fragile Islands

The lake at Tyngsjo Vildmark freezes from November to March.
We can glide across molecules so attracted they stick together,
solid edge to edge. Icy frost-quakes boom beneath its surface,
ricochet into the forest where wolves with amber eyes stare
unblinking into blizzards, or lie curled with their noses tucked
into thick long fur. Brown bears hibernate in dens with their cubs.
Solitary moose amble shyly between pines leaving depressions
in the snow where they sleep. Wolverines are here too, underground
in shelters with their stash of frozen food and family.
Their crusher jaws can bite through bone.

In the peaty blackness of the lake bed fish stay suspended,
blind and unmoving all winter long

until thaw   spills and melts   islands

form
slip away
ripples   tremble

sun
splinters
greenish
downwards

                 soon
                              midges

hover

                                       dance

              perhaps

Escape Chute

In a blur of chlorinated droplets
I sit with my small daughter
on a mat,
waiting for the attendant
to tell us *Go!*

We're adrift together
in a meandering
watery limbo
falling
through fluorescent
red
and yellow
plastic tubes
careening
into misty bends.

My daughter squeals –
and it's nothing like her sobbing
as her father flails and shouts
in the middle of our living room –

I hug her body into mine
lean further for the fun of it
knowing nothing
can happen to us here.

It's raining
and we're a stream
becoming rapids
a slippery swoosh

rushing
with a force that takes us under

'til
up we bob ecstatic!
And I hold her high
in the daylight.

Eating Chips at Tooting Bec Lido

The man in the cafe is serving the customers all on his own.
He's frying the chips, cooking falafel, chopping up salads,
dolloping ice cream on cones and sticking in flakes.

We watch from the end of the queue.
All bathers in costumes, shorts and bikinis, arms folded,
shivering in sun. Fresh from the shocking blue pool.

The smell of the chips keeps us in the line.
We taste them each time they waft past,
steeped in ketchup and salt.

YOU'RE THE LAST! bellows the man in the cafe
into the face of a man in green shorts
as he hands him a lolly.

He shouts this each time someone gets to the counter.
But we're still here in the queue.
He's still pouring chips in the fryer.

It's like he's on stage and we are the audience.
His hair flying up, face dripping, green stripy apron,
tea towel for flicking.

He half slips on a spilt chip.
Slapstick!
We laugh undercover, raise our eyes at each other.

Then we get to the front and he cooks us our chips
and we love his complaining and scowling,
dare to ask him for sauce.

Relish our time leaning on the Formica
with the man in the cafe as he dishes up
what we most want.

We grin our goodbyes,
find a spot on sunburnt grass,
savour the sting of vinegar on greasy chips.

In a queue at the exit peeling off wristbands, fumbling for keys,
we don't see the man emerge from a changing hut
wearing speedos and goggles,

until the splash as he dives into the clear, blue Lido.
We watch all agog, as he swims underwater
like a seal.

Different Strokes

As the flood water rose in Kendall,
he peeled off his clothes
and plunged into his kitchen.

Pulling his body through the dirty deluge

        amongst the jar of Branston pickle,

    floating kettle,

            empty vodka bottles,

he kicked up a storm at his cupboards.

A quick backstroke butterfly to the sink,
a short crawl to the fridge
and then some steady breaststroke

somersaulting
           at each turn touching
his carefully laid granite tiles.

Bullish

I got to know their boyish habits,
where they liked to loiter in the sun.

Four-square frames planted
on bumpy, hardened ground,

heads lowered, tails flicking,
brown Southdown faces chomping

circles with their plate-like rubber mouths.
One scratching its head

on a hawthorn branch in flower,
deliciousness in the white of its eye.

Cowpats everywhere,
crusted like pies.

Now, mud tyre tracks stain the road
leading from the field.

A metal herding pen is flung open.
They aren't behind the trees

or drinking at the stream
or sauntering in twos and threes

across the middle
twitching the yellow plastic tags

in each of their ears,
their bullish bodies grown.

Passing Through Richmond Park to Visit My Daughter

In the park you'll find a leaflet about butterflies
that live amongst the grasslands.

Butterflies with wings of softest blue and brown,
marbled, or white spots with black rims
like eyes that wake you frightened in the night.

I looked for butterflies that year, held the leaflet
in my hands, folding and unfolding it
as though expecting them to flutter out.

I don't remember seeing one.
There were groups of deer in big extended families,
with everyone accounted for

and in September, after the culling began,
a white stag ran beside my car
heat steaming off its back, stumbling and ragged.

I felt their presence in my body then,
and every time I stepped onto the ward,
a witness to my daughter's metamorphosis.

A Present from Emily Dickinson

Rain slices my face.
Traffic spatters fathomless, filthy puddles.
A pigeon hobbles on stump legs.

It's early December in Camberwell
but so far from Christmas
and nothing I would ever want.

Through the revolving hospital door
along a corridor expressionless,
I find these words

"Hope" is the thing with feathers -
That perches in the soul . . .
And never stops – at all –

I carry them to my frail chick.
Drop them on the blanket
she's wrapped around herself.

Next day she's dressed
in her gold striped t-shirt,
looking at a book of poems.

Pale sun glances the frosted window
and I can barely see.

Long Weekend

He'd been dreaming as he woke.
A puzzling one of ships adrift
which quickly disappeared
as he remembered,
his wife had gone to Paris
for the weekend.
Unused to being on his own
with no set plans

he thought he'd travel too.
Take in a garden centre –
buy a cyclamen for Sally.
He missed the turning,
pulled up opposite the huge, blank figure
of the Long Man of Wilmington,
Nordic walking towards him.

Up close he found how frayed he was,
his outline broken up by grass,
his surface interspersed with weeds.
He wasn't made of chalk
but breeze blocks painted white,
and flaking.
He badly needed tending,
it was obvious.

Turning back, he had a funny feeling
the Long Man was following him.
Chuckling, he tuned the radio
to eighties hits,
sang along to 'Gold'.
At the junction to the A27,
he glimpsed the Long Man
sat beside him.

A quiet settled, lasting
the rest of Saturday
and into Sunday.
He read the papers,
drank some beer.
Put the cricket on,
nodded off in front of the TV,
his muddy boots on the polished surface
of the coffee table.

The Long Man helped him
mend the shed.
Clear the loft.
Chop some kindling.
Light a bonfire.

He left on Sunday afternoon.
Hurdling his neighbour's fence,
taking huge strides
across gardens,
roads
and fields.
His footsteps making imprints
in the earth.

Weaving the Tails

She can see a shadow like a sea serpent
in the corner of her eye.

When she turns her head it slides
just out of focus but doesn't go away.

Her husband takes her to A & E.
They sit on orange plastic chairs

joined unnaturally together
for five hours.

Luckily, she's brought the blanket
she is crocheting.

While they wait, she hooks stitches
twirling, looping, linking, catching

cluster
      chain
           slip
                drop

stares at posters on the walls,
gauges the tension, weaves in the tails.

The blanket falls in woolly pleats
wrapping her knees snugly
in the patterns she knows by heart,

the muted corals and teal blues
which are her favourites now.

Coo-ee

I think I hear you call me at the beach today Mum,
as twin groups of starlings scud the vanishing point,
a gull as big as the sun coasts,

and *a lovely drop of sunshine* splashes on the sea.
Your words as you'd turn your face upwards,
close your eyes,

let yourself sink into the canvas of the deckchair,
your knobbly hands at rest in the stripy well of your apron.

The sea rises and breaks,
                         changing tides, inching nearer.

Symbiosis
(for Dad)

Even on the bleakest day when earth and sky
streak watercolour grey,
the bay at Weymouth
sustains its gentle rhythm,
no jagged rocks to crash against
or churning currents around protruding piers.

Even on the roughest days,
when waves erupt in force and verve
something in their landing,
perhaps the touch
of sand
and pebble,
is like an argument
started out in froth
and foam, spitting violent words,
that suddenly evaporates in misty spray,
breaks on the accepting shoreline of the bay.

Rivulets rush seawards
over broken shells
and flotsam,
building
to a pattern
where shore and sea each time agree
to recognise each other's strengths,
repeating *I am always here for you.*

Merry-Go-Round

That time we went to the beach
and couldn't stop laughing.

You covered my feet with pebbles,
I wore your sunglasses

and wispy clouds turned gold.
The sea had a wicked sparkle,

the sky was hilarious blue,
there were kittens riding horses,

penguins moving to the bandstand beat
and far out,

flowers with their petals splayed
caught the breeze and waved.

Fragile Islands is Christine Hollywood's debut collection, and joint winner of the Indigo First Poetry Competition 2023.

Indigo Dreams Publishing Ltd
24, Forest Houses
Cookworthy Moor
Halwill
Beaworthy
Devon
EX21 5UU
www.indigodreamspublishing.com